The Journey

Also by Alice Taylor

Memoirs

To School Through the Fields
Quench the Lamp
The Village
Country Days
The Night Before Christmas
The Parish

Poetry

The Way We Are
Close to the Earth
Going to the Well

Fiction

The Woman of the House
Across the River
House of Memories

Essays

A Country Miscellany

Diary

An Irish Country Diary

Children's

The Secrets of the Oak

ALICE TAYLOR

THE JOURNEY

NEW AND SELECTED POEMS

BRANDON

First published in Britain and Ireland in 2009 by Brandon
an imprint of Mount Eagle Publications
Dingle, Co. Kerry, Ireland, and
Unit 3, Olympia Trading Estate, Coburg Road, London N22 6TZ, England

www.brandonbooks.com

ISBN 9780863223914

2 4 6 8 10 9 7 5 3 1

Cover design: Anú Design
Cover Painting: *Sous les Lauriers* (1911) by Xavier Bricard, 19th–20th century
© Ulster Museum 2008; photograph reproduced courtesy the Trustees of
National Museums Northern Ireland.
Typesetting by Red Barn Publishing, Skeagh, Skibbereen

To Lena and Vincent as they begin their journey

Contents

Part One

THE HOME PLACE

Close to the Earth

Come to a quiet place,
A place so quiet
That you can hear
The grass grow.
Lie on the soft grass,
Run your fingers
Through the softness
Of its petals
And listen:
Listen to the earth,
The warm earth,
The life pulse
Of us all.
Rest your body
Against its warmth;
Feel its greatness,
The pulse and throb,
The foundation
Of the world.
Look up into the sky,
The all-embracing sky,
The canopy of heaven.
How small we really are:
Specks in the greatness

But still a part of it all.
We grow from the earth
And find
Our own place.

A Ploughed Field

Oh brown ploughed field,
What an ancient skill
Is in your turned sod,
A skill inherited
By generations of earthy men.
Beneath the sheltering trees
You cover the hillside
In a cloak of brown velvet.
What a softness is yours;
You are an open book
Yet to be written;
The virginity of the upturned sod
Waiting to be fertilised
By the hands of man
And nurtured by the warmth of nature.

A School Friend

We walked to school
Through the dew-drenched fields,
Meeting where our paths crossed
At the foot of a grassy hill.
If one ran late, the other
Left a stone message
On a mossy bridge.
He had muddy boots,
A jumper torn by briars
And hair that went its own way.
Trivial details to a mind
That raced amongst the clouds
And followed rabbits down brown burrows.
Gentle hands, twisted by a bad burning,
Reached out towards the birds,
And they perched on his fingers
At ease with one of their own.
Blessed with a mind that ran free
From the frailties of his body,
He walked during his quiet life
Close to the gates of heaven.

Stored Summer

Bridal hedges of whitethorn
Cascade on to green fields.
Under bulging wings
The gliding bees
Collect their nectar,
Bearing it back
To humming hives.

Extraction time,
The pregnant combs
Release their ripened treasure,
Golden liquid pouring
Into sparkling jars.

In a deep cupboard
Spirit of warm days
Brings to barren winter
The taste of whitethorn honey.

Earth Woman

She was as real
As the dark brown
Bank of tiered turf
With the promise
Of warmer days.
She was as solid
As a great oak,
Unbending with
The winds that blow.
She was as strong
As the hard rocks
That weather the
Crushing waves.
Her core had
The luxuriant glow
Of the black, rich,
Sensuous soil.

Going to the Well

She lifts the bucket
Of clear spring water
From the deep brown well.
Before she rests it
On the flat stone outside,
The well has refilled,
Gurgling up from the
Bowels of the earth,
Refreshed by use
Like her own pool
Of creativity.

Countrywoman

Two buckets balanced you
As you drew feed to farm animals;
Hands a map of ravines and ridges
Reflected your farm.
You bought land and held boundaries
Against grabbing neighbours.
Each night you knelt to say your prayers
To a god who demanded as much of you
As you did of yourself.

Breaking

Yielding to pressure
Beneath the forcing bucket,
The water breaks with a sob,
Fills with a gulp,
Overflows and drowns.

Wandering Walk

Evening of haze
Laden with summer smells.
Yellow woodbine darned
Through a clustered hedge.
I lift its draping fragrance
To find beneath the tangled veins
And latticed leaves
A mossy dome-shaped nest
Full of fluttering baby birds.
I carry home
Through the warm blue night
The soft swish of silken wings
And the smell of God's earth.

Shawls of Silence

Let me creep down
A brown burrow,
Down into the
Quiet womb of the earth.
Deep down where there
Is only silence.
Down, down,
Where velvet darkness
Clothes the ragged mind
In a shawl of gentle stillness.

Mikey

With soft hands you caressed my hair
And touched my face with child kisses.
Looking into your eyes of love
I saw inside
The tabernacle of the Lord.
Special child, you are so loved
That no earthly doubts
Have touched your saintly essence.
Leaving heaven's gate ajar
You live within a beam
Untouched by man.
May the world move gently with you
As you walk above its roughness.

Young Pain

When I was young
I crashed into stone walls
And broke my heart.
"Easy," adults cautioned, "easy,"
But I flew to the peaks of joy and
Dazzled by the sun hit unseen rocks,
Crashing into pools of black despair.
Flailing around in adolescent waters
I ecstasied and agonised,
Finally floating into calmer ways
Where life became more bearable,
But never again as beautiful.

Chains

Saw a bird
Upon a tree,
Smiled at him.
He sang to me:
"Will you come today,
Come with me and fly away
Across the silent ocean wide,
Over yawning mountainside?
You will see the things that be,
That thrill my heart
And make me free."
But I said, "I have things to do
So I cannot fly with you."
He looked at me
In a sad way
And sang, "You cannot fly today.
Because you're busy doing things
You will never fly on wings.
You cannot soar above the sound;
You belong on solid ground."

Beneath a Tree

I lie on the grass
Beneath a tree,
The sky peeps down
Through the leaves at me;
It's cool in here
On this warm day,
A pale green haven
In the sun's hot ray.
I see a nest
Away up there,
Twigs interlaced
With horse's hair,
Firm built for
Fledglings' wear,
In a branch's arm
Of nature's care.
Now a butterfly
Sails into view,
Its white wings
Edged in delicate blue;
Then a bee
From the hives near by,
Buzzing hello
As he passes by.

Fluttering through
The branches above,
On its way to rest
Comes a soft grey dove.
Its eyes peer down
With a solemn stare
As if to ask
What are you doing here?
Then deciding
To wait and see,
Its cooing voice
Serenading me.
A summer's day
Beneath a tree.

Dreams on the Wing

Dreams are the wings of life;
They take you over the clouds,
But to dream you fly alone,
And wing away from the crowd.
As a bird of the air you soar
And climb to the heights of delight,
Then glide back down to earth
Refreshed by the vision of light.
In the mind are folded wings
You open and fly to the stars;
Dreams are a wondrous gift
Not trapped by human bars.

Inside

Pool of creativity
Our divine roots
Link with creation
In womb of earth
Where wings sprout
To fly to the peaks
Of ecstasy.

A Memory

The waste ground was choked with weeds
That grew above her head,
But in the middle of this bloomed
One flower of golden red.
The little child came every day
To gaze upon the scene.
The flower it was the loveliest sight
That she had ever seen.

This flower took root and blossomed.
It grew inside her head
And led her on to lovely things
Long after it was dead.

A Great Tree

You stand there
In splendid isolation.
A remote stillness
Centred in a green field,
Your praying arms
Held forth
In majestic supplication.
Shrouded in your
Green leafy depths,
What a tranquil, untouchable
World of nature
You portray.

A Touch of Spring

Spring came today
And walked with me
Up the hill,
Breathing softness in the air,
Opening gates within my head.
The birds felt his presence,
Pouring forth symphonies
Of unrestrained welcome.
It was mid-January
And he just came
To have a peep,
Trailing behind him
Along the valley
Wisps of purple veils.

The Mind's Eye

To have seen
With the mind's eye
Things to be written
Before you die.
Within your head
A subconscious shelf
Of details indexed
By another self.
Always there,
A second mind,
Ever probing
The scenes behind.
Beneath the swift
And flowing tide
An inner depth,
Another side.
Mosses trail
As waters flow,
Roots grow buried
Deep below.

Back to Simplicity

Clergyman all dressed in black,
What a mighty church is at your back.
We are taught that by your hand
We must be led to our promised land.
Jesus is locked in your institutions
Of ancient laws and resolutions,
Buried so deep and out of sight
Sometimes we cannot see the light,
Behind huge walls that cost so much
Where simple things are out of touch.
But could it be He's not within
These walls so thick, with love so thin?
Does He walk on distant hills
Where long ago He cured all ills?
Is He gone out to open places
To simple people, all creeds all races?
Is Jesus gone from off the altar,
Catching fish down by the water?
Is He with the birds and trees,
Gathering honey with the bees?
Could it be in this simple way
That God meant man to kneel and pray?

Earth Mantra

Garden spade
Easing open
Brown earth,
Creating crevices
Into darkness,
Light softening
Compressed layers.

Mantra spade
Rooting mind
Into earth.

Healing Place

The frosty, feathery grass
Crunched beneath my feet
As my warm valley
Caressed me in welcome;
Bejewelled with frost
The trees and grass
Sparkled in the morning sun
And across the river
The mothering mountains
Shrouded in a misty light
Stood ground. Not a sound
But the gurgling of the river
And, companions of the solitary,
My feathered friends
Echoing my thoughts
Pour forth their ecstasy
In unrestrained delight.

To hold these thoughts
And this beloved place
So much part of me
For ever in my mind.

I let this balm of my growing
Soak into my inmost soul,
To be written
On the back pages
Of my mind,
To be re-read
In some distant hour
When my need may be great
And I can no longer
Come to this my healing place.

Free to be Children

Give our children
Time to be children,
To savour the wonder
That is theirs.
To blossom in the world
Of their simplicity,
Not darkened
By the shadows
That are ours.

Let them bask
In the warmth
Of their sunshine,
Cleanse in the
Softness of their tears,
Be kissed by the
Beauties of nature,
Let them free
In the kingdom
That is theirs.

Their beauty
Is the purity
Of heaven,

Not tainted
By the ugliness
Of man.
Let's not destroy
Their simplicity.
We never can
Improve
On what they have.

Please Don't

Don't put money
In my Christmas stocking.
Don't take away my fun.
I believe in magic moments;
Don't put clouds across my sun.
My life is full of golden wonders,
Heaven's rays still beam on me,
Let me weave my golden dreams,
Leave me my joy of make-believe.
Fairies dance on silver dewdrops
Tossing gold dust through my days,
My golden days are so happy
Don't dark them with your grown-up ways.

The Men with Scythes

When the graveyard became overgrown
And headstones were buried in grass
Then they came,
The men with scythes,
Weather-beaten farming men
Who worked steadily
At their own pace,
Edged and cut
With the calm determination
Of those who endlessly
Work the fields.
The crack of blade on stone
Brought forth blessings
On the dead;
Uncovering the resting place
Of an old friend
Stirred forgotten memories.
As the moon rose
Behind the steeple
Order was restored
And headstones stood
Proud and free,
The living giving
Dignity to the dead.

Cow Dung

As a child my feet felt
The three stages of cow dung:
First, warm green slop oozed up
Between pressing toes,
Poulticed sinking heels.
Later sap fermented
Beneath a black crust,
Resisted a probing toe.
Then hard grey patch,
Dehydrated and rough
Beneath tender soles,
Its moisture absorbed
Into growing fields.

Noble cow dung fed the earth
Which gave us our daily bread.

A Scratching Pole

Cows eased
Their arched backs
And unreachable places
On rough-hewn poles
In hilly fields.
A simple thing
That brought comfort
To dumb animals.
Now the poles are gone.
Do the cows no longer
Need to scratch their backs?

In a Small Field

Two cows
Exchanged neck massage,
Exuding contentment:
Bovine bliss on a summer's day.

Nobody Told the Cows

The cattle seek
A sheltering hedge,
Instinct leading them
Away from cold winds;
But the hedge is gone
And now they stand by
An electric fence,
Cold rains slashing
Their exposed rumps.

Forgotten Cows

Grass long gone
From their bare allotment.
Now they endlessly
Traverse the muddy ground
And bellow with hunger
As they stretch desperately
For glowing rich grass
Beyond the electric fence.

Fresh Flowers

Give me a bunch
Of dew-fresh flowers,
What if they will not last?
I cannot live in the future;
The present is all I ask.

Bonded

She is old and tired,
He a strong man of the land,
Smelling of cows and open fields.
He raises her gently with hands
That have lifted a newborn calf
And placed it beneath its mother's head
For her to lick away the film of birth.
Now he rests his frail mother
On her final bed, where death
Will lick away the mantle of life.

The Waiting

Death hid behind her chair,
But we left her
To steal out into a moist green wood
Where pine and hazel filled the air
With wild freedom.
Long grass fell across our feet
In strands of trailing cobwebs.
We needed that day
Of filtering sun
And laughing birds
To light up the nights
While we waited for death
To emerge from behind her chair.

The Long Night

It is morning.
The grey dawn seeps in,
The fire whispers,
The clock ticks.
My mother's aged face on the pillow
Is tranquil now.
She is weary of long days and nights
Of monotonous inactivity,
Waiting for deliverance
On the welcome wings of death.
But they waft past
And she sighs,
"It's not easy to die."

Reversed Roles

Long-legged exuberant grandson
Lifts her easily into her pillowed bed,
Laughing merrily at her complaints.
Casting aside her sadness,
She smiles fondly at his happy ways.
She had changed his napkins
And filled his childish days with love.
The roles are reversed
And she needs him now.

Uplift

"Fruit of the earth
And work of human hands."
Today I heard
And saw
For the first time
The earth
The human
The divine.

Words

Words
Are messengers of thought,
A brush
Which on the canvas paints
A picture
That reflects the mind.
I pen these words
To paint my thoughts
Upon the pages here within:
Gently absorb
The scenes you find:
You have crossed the threshold
Of my mind.

Walk the Fields

When I go home
I walk the fields,
The quiet fields
Where the warm dew
Had squelched between
My childish toes.
To sit beneath
The cool oak and ash
That sheltered
My adolescent dreams.
These trees stand
With leafy arms
Outstretched
Like lovers',
Not in passion
But with gentle
Sighs of contentment.
I watch the cows
Graze peaceful
Beside the river
Curving its way
Through furzed inches
Into the woods beyond.

This is a holy place
Where men have worked
Close to God's earth
Under the quiet heavens.

Goodbye, House

Vacuum womb house,
Contracted into a new life,
An afterbirth remaining,
Whispers and shadows
Of another day.
Memory on its
Soft grey clouds
Wafting through the rooms,
Webbing here
The part of me
That belongs.
The living that was blended
Through these stones,
So I take with me
Past soul of this house
And leave behind
Part of mine.

Looking Forward

The joy of
Anticipation,
Awaiting dreams'
Realisation;
Looking forward
Is the fun
Of happy things
Yet to come.

Part Two

THE WISEING YEARS

The Wiseing Years

You were unburnished gold
That polished warm
With the living years;
I had loved you
With a young girl's
Delectable fancy,
But the wiseing years
Revealed your inner depth.
You have wrapped me
In the warm blankets
Of your love,
Your comforting arms
Sheltering me from
Life's icy draughts,
Warming our togetherness,
Creating in our life
An inner glow.

Love

Because you believed
I would light up your life,
I did.
Because you believed
I could do anything,
I did.
Because you think
I am filled with love,
I am.
Because you think
I am beautiful,
I am.

Because you know
I will walk on water,
I will.
Because you know
I will reach for the stars,
I will.

Love enabled me
To do the undoable,
To reach the unreachable,
To attain the unattainable.

It was the combination
That unlocked the vault
Hidden within.

Complete

Making love
You span mountains
Walk on treetops
Swim in the sea mist
Of your mind.

Making love
A fusion of
Inner and outer being,
An explosion of tranquillity
That is complete.

Golden Flower

Tender, beautiful love,
A golden sunflower
Deep-rooted in the earth
Within my heart,
Kissed by the warm rays
Of him who gave it life.
I lay no claim or right
To this golden flower;
It is a bonus to my life,
Growing in the walled garden
Of my heart.
And when winter falls
Within my mind
I withdraw to this sunny place
And warm my frozen thoughts
In the embracing radiance
Of this golden flower.

Communion

Warm bodies
Close together
Kindling feelings
Deep within,
Fanned by memories
Of former ecstasies.
Close friends
And lovers,
Mind, heart
And body
Joined in harmony,
Complete communion
Of human kind.

The Honey Tree

The day was soft and mellow,
Growth was in the ground;
I went into the garden,
Climbed to the honey sound,
Eased my spade through the fallen leaves
Of golden brown and red
And as I lifted out the earth
I made a soft brown bed.
Mother nature opened wide
Her arms of velvet brown
And on her maternal lap
I sat my young tree down.
All around the soft young roots
I folded mother earth
And when my baby tree stood tall
I felt joy as in a birth.
I tied her to a firm stake
To hold her in the sways,
A seasoned piece of older wood
To guard her growing days.

Jacky's Garden

Here there is no set layout,
Nature's freedom is all about.
A garden cared by loving hands,
Green profusion with nothing planned

Flowers and fruit freely abound;
Bees in their hives hum a mellow sound;
No regimented hedges in orderly array:
This is a garden with nature's sway.

A haven created by a man of love,
Man of the earth, with thoughts of above;
Here nature, love and care combine
To create a refuge, an escape from time.

A Neighbourhood

Be kind
When you talk
Of me
With your friends.
Our public image
Is a light
Shining
From our rooftop:
Do not shatter it
With a steel-pointed arrow.
Fragmented glass
Breaks
Other images,
So let all lights
Shine
And make this
A warm place
For living.

Battered Chalice

God's day,
The bird and sun
Celebrate his creation.
You pick daisies
With such joy in your hands;
Little child in the body of a man,
You are the host
In a battered chalice.
"*Daoine le Dia*," old people said,
And how wise they were
Because you live within
The circle of God's arm;
Not for you
The snares of this world.
You walk above man's narrow vision.

The Elms

We had walked
Where you had stood
And this is a meaner place
For your going.
You had grown
To elegant supremacy,
Lending grandeur
To our village.
You have been
Because a man
Looked to the future,
And we inherited.
Let us likewise
Leave behind us
Roots in the soil
Of Innishannon,
So that our children
May walk beneath
The shelter
Of our foresight.

Jim

Just across the road
Jim lived in a shed;
It wasn't very big,
Just enough to hold his bed.
He was never lonely,
He chatted on the street,
A kindly neighbour fed him
So he had enough to eat.
But it didn't seem right
Him sleeping in the cold;
Something should be done
As Jim was getting old.
So he went into a home
Where everything was right
And everyone felt good
Now Jim was in by night.
But when I went to see him
His face a story told;
His body was dry and warm
But his eyes were lost and cold.
Jim had lived here too long
To dig up his ancient roots;
His body now had comfort
But his heart was in his boots.

Jim died in September,
Died in a spotless bed,
But he had died six months before,
The day he left the shed.

The Wall

Six rows deep they stand at the wall:
Men with flowing beards and fur hats,
Mysterious men in long black coats.
Apart from their beautiful women
With olive skins and raven hair, they prayed,
Elegant and dignified they swayed
Backwards and forwards,
Hands pressed against their wall,
With closed eyes and intense faces.

Jesus, are you with them in their wall?
We believe you are in our host.
They believe you are yet to come.
We believe you came,
But before either of us thought anything
You were.

Why Here, Lord?

Why did you come to this arid land,
Heat-bleached and sun-soaked,
Where camels grind their teeth
And volcanic tempers can sizzle
Into an eruption of violence?

Did you never consider
Coming as a Kerryman?
Kerry is moist and green
And they have many donkeys.
Mary could have ridden one
And made the flight into Cork
From your kingdom in Kerry.

Perhaps they expected you in Kerry
When they christened it the Kingdom.

Peter's Field

You were full of enthusiasm
Laced with human weakness.
But because of your great heart
Jesus made you shepherd of his flock.
When we gathered in your field
On the shores of Galilee
You drew us together under a shady tree
With rocks for seats around a little table.
A warm breeze caressed our faces
And flowers and fruits of your fertile valley
Filled the air with their fragrance.
Then when we were ready
You brought your friend Jesus.

Emigrants

We will come home
When the children are older;
We will come home
When they finish school;
We will come home when they settle.

But the time was never right
And the dream was for ever
Just beyond their fingertips.

Tribes

So easy to step
Into your world
But would I ever
Be free of mine,
And coming back
Would I ever be
Free of yours?

Turn Down the Sound

Background music was the start
Of this all-prevailing sound;
It began as a soother,
Now it vibrates through the ground.
In the solitude of the great outdoors
Hear the music of the waves,
But the harmony is shattered
By transistors' howling wails.
Silence is broken:
We can no longer hear
The whispering of our mind
For the thunder in our ear.

Shreds of Hope

You came
Shrouded in shreds
Of fragile hope.
Beneath them
Your sorrow
Lurked in shadows.

But your
Strands of hope
Will weave
A warm cloak
And you will
Walk again.

Togetherness

Forced apart
By busy days
We who belong
Together,
As the interlaced
Fingers
Of praying
Hands,
Join again
In quiet times
At peace
In our
Togetherness.

Watch It

Looked in the mirror
And I was there,
Ugly and sour-faced
With greasy hair.
And I asked myself,
Where have you gone?
What thorny bush
Have you sat upon?
And I said to myself,
Get off your butt
And pull yourself out
Of your poor-me rut.

The Waterfall

Came to the wood
With ragged mind.
The soothing waterfall
Washed through my tight head
Stiff neck
Knotted stomach,
Coursed out
Through my toes,
Carrying my garbage
Down into the river.

Birth Joy

On the first day
Of the new year
You were born
Perfect and beautiful,
Ahead of schedule
But complete.
The agony
Of labour pains
Climaxing
In the joy
Of perfection achieved,
A little girl
The crowning glory.
Tears unrestrained
Poured on your
Downy head,
You were baptised
In streams of joy.

Regrowth

Father and daughter
Laugh and argue;
He opens the gate
Of his world to her.
She has some of the love
That once was mine
And I am glad
That like a garden
We have flowered
Into a new growth.

Mothering

Awake half the night
Soothing teenage tears,
Listening to splintered emotions.
In another room
A sullen non-talker
Head buried in pillow.

Come morning:
"Why did you listen
Last night?"
From the other:
"Where were you
When I wanted to talk last night?"

Mother's place is in the wrong.

Parenting

We look down
Sunlit pathways,
Willing our children
To travel there.
But they turn
Into unsighted ways,
Travel through
Deep undergrowth,
And we worry
About their journey
As we watch
The sun go down
On our horizons.

Own Wings

My precious daughter,
Poised for flight
From the top branch
Of your childhood tree,
Eager to test your wings:
Wait until you can fly alone
Lest you become a passenger
On another's flight
And never know the glory
Of free flying
Or feel the challenge
Of your wings against the wind.

The Young

You spawn them
Into unknown distances
And watch their
Vulnerabilities crash
On jagged rocks.
Too wild for calm
And shallow pools
They leap the rapids
To find their place
Beyond your vision.

Tortured Teens

I pen these words
To record the tears
And the tortures
Of the teenage years.
Being a teenager
Is sometimes rough;
Being a teenager's parent
Is twice as tough.
When times are good
They're with their peers;
When they want to gripe
Then they reappear.
Home is the place
To let it all out.
They grunt and grouse
Or just lay about.
I look at this son
Who behaves like a mule.
I think, dear Lord,
Have I reared a fool?
When they are grown
Will I still be around?
Wish patience was something
I could buy by the pound.

But I've got to draw
From resources within
And often I think
My resources are thin.
Sometimes I ask
Will I ever survive?
When teens are behind
Will I still be alive?

If in the years
That are yet to come,
I'll look back in memory
And dream these were fun,
This poem will be here
To bring truth to mind
And make me be glad
Tortured teens are behind.

Rejuvenation

Swirls of steam shroud the tired body
Of an old, old woman.
I crawl feebly over the bath edge
And submerge into the sudsy warmth.
My children are parasites
My husband unloving,
My friends demanding;
I want to die.
My body dissolves,
My mind evaporates,
I become nothing,
Drifting into oblivion.
A few hot-water top-ups
And an hour later
I come back together.
My children are independent,
My husband adoring,
My friends supportive;
It's good to be alive,
And I high-step
Out of the bath
Vibrant and beautiful,
And the old lady

With all her problems
Disappears down
The plughole.

Then

Early spring morning,
Nobody on the beach.
We came searching
For oiled birds
And found only
Sparkling sunbeams
Riding bareback
On leaping waves,
A sunlit world
Alive with sea music.
It was a picture
To be painted
When the scene was fresh;
I cannot
Now recall
All the magic
That was then.

Get Me Out of Here!

Oh! the pain of this city street
The crowd
The noise
And the burning heat.
Oh! the joy of a mossy stream
Cool grass
Tall trees
And no human being.

Inner Sanctum

Let me steal five minutes
To welcome in the dawn,
To touch its dewy fingers
As they creep across the lawn,
To watch beneath a misty tree
The sun roll back the night,
Its beams transforming darkness
With soft translucent light,
To hear the birds awake
With delight to meet their day.
Let their happiness infuse me
To meet my day their way;
Let this tranquil scene give balance
To the busy day ahead,
To create a tranquil pool
For withdrawal inside my head.

A Rusty Love Affair

In a sun-baked shed
With black-grained hands,
These iron men of steam
Sweat oil pursuing an ideal.
There she sits in state,
This queen of the past,
Waiting for her archaic
Limbs to be greased
Into motion, her joints
Soothed gently by her
Black lovers, unquestioning
In their complete adoration.
In this brown station yard
Carriages grey with old age,
Retired queens proudly wear
The grandeur of another day.
Here, a dream in creation,
An old train being reborn
When men become gods
Breathing life into dead iron.

Old Dresser

Slowly, tediously,
Dead layers of paint
Are scraped away,
A technicolour
Combination
Of many coats.
Then rebirth,
As pale skin
Of the original
Breaks through.
A wondrous moment
When she stands naked
In her pine perfection.

Clinging

Do not cling
To him
As ivy
To a tree,
Draining his strength,
Growing nothing
Of your own:
Stand tall and free,
Then you will grow
As two strong trees
Sheltering each other,
Your roots intertwining.

No Time

I am old,
I live alone;
Please don't leave me
On my own.
I sit on a chair,
I lie in bed.
Voluntary services keep me fed.
This is where I would be
But please, please call on me.
The clock goes tick
The clock goes tock.
Please turn that key
That's in the lock.
The time is long,
The time is slow;
Long hours alone,
I'm feeling low.
Please come
And chat awhile,
The human touch
Will make me smile.

Terrible Tidy

The old stone wall
Wore a saddle of ivy.
A screaming strimmer
Stripped it bare.
A demented robin circled
Her shredded home and babies.

Gap In Time

"Come at 5 o'clock," she said.
I had expected it to be three,
So I had two gift hours;
Not enough to do anything,
Just a gap in time.
I made a cup of tea
And lay on the couch
With a copy of Ted Hughes.
For two hours
I shared his life
And I came back to my own
Under his halo of genius.

It is through gaps in time
Wondrous moments enter.

Poor Me!

I know I must not
Get up-tight;
I must relax
And see things right.
People put my nerves
On edge,
Between my eyes
They drive a wedge.
A heavy load
Is on my back,
A pony carrying
A horse's pack.
Tension a knot
Within my head,
Tightened by something
Somebody said.
Snapped at a remark
I should have let pass;
Think I'm becoming
A pain in the ass.

Unforgiven Thief

She spoke to me
From ravaged mid-life eyes:
"I was sexually abused at six;
It went on for a long time.
Where was my mother then?
The bastard stole my childhood
Sullied everything clean in me
Savaged my unborn sexuality.
May he rot in hell for ever.
The joy of forgiveness
Can never bloom for me:
He brutally destroyed
The innocence of my soul.
An eternity of misery
Is not too great a payment
For a burnt-out childhood
And a lifetime of scorched memories."

Revenge

Your sin was black,
Unforgivable and unforgettable,
But you crawled out of the cesspit
And painfully picked away your filth.
You must have hoped
That your sin would be forgiven.

But we have not forgotten
And now we come for healing
With your destruction in mind.
When you are destroyed
Will we feel better?

Crippling Memory

A deep wound of childhood
Buried in the recesses of her mind
Lay sleeping for many years.
When similar circumstances arose
A disturbed giant awoke
And walked down
The laneways of her mind
To cripple the present.

Three Sorrows

The first,
A blighting
Of an inner bud
Suffered in silence.

The second,
A tragedy
Eased by the cloak
Of public sympathy.

The third,
Unveiling of a sin
Viewed with revulsion.
Unkindest cut of all.

Millennium

Was it the moment when the last light faded?
Was it the moment when the clock struck twelve?
Was it the moment we all sang together?
No! it waited until I was at last alone.

I Was Happy Then

A sunny morning,
Running barefoot
Through dew-drenched grass
Picking buttercups:
I was happy then.

Wedding evening,
Together on a train
Thundering into the future,
Alone at last:
I was happy then.

A delivery ward,
Muzzy with exhaustion,
Holding a little girl,
Perfection achieved:
I was happy then.

Holding in my hand
My very own book;
My thoughts realised,
Dreams in substance:
I was happy then.

Hanging on the wall
My painting in oils,
Easy on the eye,
A wish realised:
I was happy then.

So many nights
Of close enchantment
With one so dear,
To be so loved:
I was happy then.

Part Three

GRIEF AND GRACE

The End or the Beginning

The room
Is cloaked in
After death
Stillness.
He is gone into
Impenetrable
Sacred silence.
We are left
Standing
On the edge
Of the great mystery.

Uprooted

From my inner grove
A deep-rooted tree
Has been dragged up.
A gaping chasm
Remains.
Where once I stood
Beneath sheltering branches,
A weeping hole
Pours black tears
From my morning
Down through my day.

Dragged

You were darned
Into the arteries
Of my every day.
Your going
Dragged sinews
From the fibre
Of my inner being.
My soul
Ran red with
Bloody pain.

Without Skin

You stripped away
The very skin
That shielded me
From the lurches
Of daily life.
Now every dent
Is felt at the core.
I walk around
A swell of
Smouldering pain.

Without Wings

A bird cut deep
At the wing knuckle
Icy air touches
Red and raw.
How long healing
And baby feathers?
Will I ever fly again?

Secrets

You are gone
So now I walk
The beach alone.
I pick up
A small round stone
Glistening with sea sand,
Massage it through my fingers.
The smooth hard stone
Withholds the secrets
Of sea and land.
Enclosed and impenetrable,
It is as incomprehensible
As death.

Parting

Years ago I came
To this place
Where I became part of you.
Now you are gone
To a place
Where you are no longer
Part of me.
Will I one day
Go to that place
Where we will be
For ever part of
Each other?

Climbing

I claw up
The black rock
Face of grief
With grim determination,
Seeking tiny footholds,
Gripping each ledge,
Because if I should slip
I fall into nothingness.

But if I keep climbing
You will be there
In the sunshine
Of wholeness.

Trapped

I awake in a steel cage
And painfully force open
Cold rigid bars
So that I can crawl
Into another bleak day.

Cold Dawn

Grey light seeps in
And the razor edge
Of realisation cuts
Through my waking mind.
The coldness of aloneness
Chills my nakedness.

Have I the courage
To reinvent myself
Because I was part
Of a whole?

The Droopy Wing

Each day
We came to the garden,
Little brown blackbird
With a droopy wing
And I with two broken wings.
She eased my hurt
As she moved gently
Examining blades of grass
And looking up at me
Waiting to be fed.

One day
She did not come.
I looked for her.
Feathers in the grove
Told of a stray cat.
My heart ached
At the savagery of life.

Wet Blanket

My first day out
After the funeral,
I walked along
The city street
Wearing a mask
Of normality.
A stranger intercepted:
"Sorry about your husband;
I buried mine ten years ago
And I want to tell you
It doesn't get any better."

At that time
I needed her
Like a hole
In the head.

Are the bereaved
A coat hanger
For others to drape
Their misery on?

Defeated

I am weary
And a cold apathy
Oozing through my bones
Makes movement meaningless;
A dead weight
Crushing my mind
Blocks my forward path
And fills my mind with grey.
I could stay here,
Motionless for ever
In a nook of forgetfulness,
Letting the mainstream course on;
And when the final flood
Would swirl the river down
I would be carried on its crest
Into the final waters beyond.

The Back Yard

Yesterday I washed the back yard
With a mind full of throbbing pain.
Scalding tears joined piped water
Through hoses that you had connected.

It is in the ordinary everyday
That I miss you most.
When all was clean and rearranged
I asked myself, "Why did I bother?"

But you were never one
To sit and moan;
You would have kept going,
And so must I

Because savage grief
Must be worked through
And grappled with hour by hour
So that one day your memory
Becomes a glorious tub of flowers.

Keeping Busy

Am I afraid to stop
In case all my pieces
Shatter apart?
Could I disintegrate
And never come back
Together again?

The Gap

We had gone
There together.
Now I went alone
And could not
Fill the space;
Wanted to go home,
To lock myself in
Where I did not
Have to hold back tears
And pretend to be normal.

Vacancy

He lived in the midst of us,
A quiet presence with a listening ear.
When he went an icy wind
Blew through the days
That he had filled with kindness.

Dark Crevices

Night weaves
A grey cobweb
That nets
The morning mind.
Overnight
Old pain creeps out
Of dark crevices.

In the morning
I must crawl
Out from under
A black blanket,
Let the light
Into my mind
And the sun
Dilute the darkness.

Fr Denis

Death had invaded him;
It was in his voice.
"A woman from Tipperary
Is dying here with us.
She will probably go today."

He would be with her
To ease her from the hospice
On to the lap of God.

Spuds

My pike lifted
A green stalk
Thrusting white spuds
Through brown earth.
A resurrection
Lighting inner being.
I came home carrying
A bucket of new spuds.

Joseph

Eased layers of dead paint
Off the old statue.
Slowly a flakey white cloak
Snowed on to the brown earth.
Portland stone emerged.
Original beauty unfolded.
My dormant spirit awoke
And winged with others
In the garden air
Around the revealed St Joseph.

A Little Healing

"Come to Writers' Week.
It might help a little."
I doubted it!

There we created
Fantasy worlds
And I left reality behind.
When I came home
A little healing
Had happened.

Write Out

The gift of writing
Eased my compressed pain.
It poured off my pen
On to the open page.

Coming!

Aloneness
Saturated
My soul
No word
No smile
No touch.
But yesterday
In creativity
Together again.

Coming a Little

Today
A small bud
Blossomed.
Uncovered
By deep
Digging.
It needs
Light.
So I must
Sit quietly
In the sun.

Coming Back

You have gone
Into the unknown.
We are on the edge
Peering into nothingness.
You have loosened our roots.
We are tilted across the divide.
We must reroot,
Struggle back,
Because our time
Is not yet come.

Afterwards

His room
A book,
The story
Of his life.
Each crevice
Filled to capacity.
A beehive
Of remembrances.

A collection
Of coins,
Family history,
Rare books
And stamps.
His room
As his life,
A book of interests.

I turned back
The pages of his life.
This man's treasures,
His love of
Such little things.

I walked on
Sacred ground
Back through
His years.

The Grief Road

A cold November day
She came in the door
Exuding warmth and comfort.
"The sun will shine again,"
She told me gently.

As we sat by a warm fire
On that frozen day
She melted for a little while
My inner ice.

She was a constant caller
Who walked with me along
The road of grief.
She had been there
And knew the way,
A friend who had learned
How to be a friend.

Escape

Be glad for me
That I shall not
Weaken and wither,
Will not be trapped
In the vagaries
Of old age.
I walked through
Spring and summer,
Savoured autumn,
Smelt the first frost
Of early winter,
Then flew on
To eternal spring.

Blended Spirit

With you my spirit died;
My laughter and sunlit days
Went into the tomb.
Black time of grief
When desolation
Dug deep ravines
Into the sanctuary
Of my soul.
One day a sunbeam crept
Between the stones and
Gently warmed my wings.
I had overwintered.
The sap of life had survived.

When I finally fluttered free
You came with me,
A new creation of blended spirit.
I will always mourn your going
But your spirit is closer now
Than when separated by the human.

Linked by Love

You are gone
And I am here
Wounded by your going,
Grieving for togetherness.
But we are more
Than we have shared.
Let not my staying
Or your going
Divide us now
Because you and I
Are closer than
Our earthly bodies.
Our love as a rainbow
Reaching over life and death
Links us now.

Glen Falls

The roaring waterfall
Blew the crust
Off the hard wound of grief.
As pain burst forth
It screamed aloud
With the raging torrents.
But the determined water
Penetrated into the depths
Of locked-up grief,
Showed no mercy.
I cried and screamed
With anger and relief
As foaming water
Washed out imprisoned pain.

When the storm abated
Icy water had cleansed
My inner being.
I was more at ease
With my deep sorrow.

Brown Poultice

Easter Saturday
Still in the tomb,
Thorns embedded
In my mind.

On a hard hill
Outside the village
We planted trees.
Dug deep holes.
Back breaking work
In freezing sleet.
But into the holes
Ran raw pain
That became absorbed
Into brown earth,
And the kind earth
Poulticed my wounds.

The Parting Touch

They came to dull your grief
With their kindness:
Big-hearted horsey men
With black forelocks
Over wise eyes.
They stood with you
And shared your hospitality,
Their comfort not needing articulation.
They were there to ease
Her going from you,
Their presence an ointment
On your wound.

Early next morning
You sat with her
In the quiet church.
As you left
You placed your hand lightly
On her varnished coffin.

Uncle Danny

He was a man
Who took life
By the throat
And demanded what was his.
Moderation was not his theme,
Rather excess in all things,
Even in the greatness
Of his heart.
You could forgive him
Many faults
Because of so great a heart.
He loved life
With the spontaneity
Of a rushing river
That could not be blocked;
And yet it was stopped short
In full flood.
My heart ached to see him
Tubed by nose and hand,
Strapped like a wild creature
In his hospital bed;
A frightened animal,
Unaccustomed to restraint,
Brought in to shelter

From the winter cold,
Eyes dilated in terror.
A man of hilly places
Trapped in antiseptic crucifixion;
Slow death dragged on for months.
This mighty man withered.
The torrent
Declined to a trickle
And then was no more.

Kindred Spirit

Your fine mind,
Uncushioned by the dullness
That makes life bearable,
Penetrated masks,
Heard the unspoken,
Saw the unseen.
On gifted wings
Your artistic imagery
Suffered and sought
Perfection beyond our horizons.

God of No Explanations

Little girl gone.
Violent eruption,
A fusion of pain,
Sucking them into
An open wound
Of weeping hurt.

Can the love
That created her
Recreate them.

Victor

Around eyes of sorrow
He arranged a forced smile.
"I no longer belong anywhere."

For over forty years
They had been a team.
Now like a male swan
He is crossing
A black lake
Alone.

Mary's Ointment

The funeral notice said
"No flowers or cards",
But the old neighbour
Did not read the paper.
He plucked two roses
From his wild bush,
Tied them tightly
With foxy binder twine
And laid them on her coffin.

Mary's sweet-smelling ointment
On the feet of Jesus.

Cobh Cortège

Like a silent tide
They carried him
Down the hill
And bore him up
The cathedral steps:
One of their own
From the roots
Of this old town.

Quietly and reverently
They flowed into
The spreading pews
And laid him
Before the high altar.

Their choice of hymn,
"How Great Thou Art",
Praised God and man.

Bereavement Mass

They sat in pews,
Rows of bereaved
In a pool of grief.
Lives crumbled by crashes,
Suicides and lingering deaths.
Their palpable suffering
Filled the church.
The road from Calvary
Has no short cuts.

Running

I did not know
It was a race,
But I ran
With all the others
Past quiet corners
Where I could have
Picked the daisies,
Past many people
I could have loved.
But there was no time
For it was a race
And the prize at the end
Was death.

Remembering Alone

A wedding anniversary
Is for two.
But yesterday for the first time
I remembered alone.
The memories of beginnings
Flooded back.

The road of togetherness
Began in joy
But now I journey
Alone in grief.

A Year On

Last year
I was part
Of the trauma.
This year it
Is reenacted
In my mind.
I go around
With a play
In my head.

Reborn

Can something
Come out of nothing?
Can light
Come out of darkness?
Since you died
I have disintegrated
Into fragments.
Can I be reborn
Out of the womb
Of your death?

Garretstown

A black pool
In my belly pit.
Tar at the bottom
Of a bucket.
Sat on a rock
By the sea
And the water
Swished and washed,
Wearing away
The base.
A gap came,
Tar leaked out,
Sea washed
The bucket
And my belly pit.

Kindness

The warmth of your kindness
Kept me in my mind;
Its worth could not be measured,
It had goodness undefined;
You held out a caring hand
When I was full of pain;
You thawed my frozen being
And made me live again.

Part Four

WINTER PLOUGHING

Come Sit Awhile

How nice to sit
And think awhile
Of little things
To make you smile,
Happy things
You did in fun
Long ago
When you were young.
To think of people
Who were kind
And left a ray
Of light behind,
People who were
Nice to know
When you were young
Long time ago.
So come and sit
With me awhile
And think of things
To make us smile.

Welcome

A long wet winter
Drowns our spirit.
With souls sodden
From sheeting rain
We welcome in
The light of spring.
Now we will rise
As birds released
From locked cages
To fly again.

Easter

Planted a lilac tree,
Gift from a friend.
It rose from the earth
Like the risen Christ.
Friendship and resurrection,
Branches of the same tree.

Sweet Pea

Rain soaked
Summer morning.
Tears glistening
On the pale pink faces
Of delicate sweet peas.
Easing back their
Curling tendrils
I carefully snip
Their fragile stems.

They arrange themselves
In an old jug
On the kitchen table,
Draping over the rim
In multicoloured profusion,
Filling the kitchen with
Their exquisite fragrance.

Changing Places

Behind my back door,
Abandoned wilted and dehydrated;
Gently I pruned your dead foliage,
Eased you into a bed of soft earth.
That long summer
You grew tall and leggy
Sometimes drooping
When you cried for water,
But before the final gasp
The watering can rescued.

Then one cold November day
Bad news burst in my front door.
I wilted and gasped
Behind my back door.
You burst into golden bloom.
I brought your sunshine
Into my kitchen
Where during bleak days
You sustained my soul.

His Dog

Every morning
He passes by,
His dog on a lead
Tail wagging.
Happy smiling pair
Sharing togetherness
On a morning stroll.

Airborne

Fingers flew
Over notes.
Soaring spirits
Winged the room.
Musical souls
Danced in the air
Above our heads.

Needless Question

Yesterday I had a
"Why did God bother?" day,
But this morning
On a windswept hill
Hundreds of crows
Soared in exultation
Against the wind.
They had no need to ask
"Why did God bother?"

Deeper

Younger
I daily laughed and cried.
Older
Tears and laughter
Run deeper.
Joys and sorrows
Have burrowed
Into my soul.

Being

As a bird on the wing I fly,
One wing in the future,
One wing in the past,
Only my head in the present.
May I bring both wings into now
So that I can live
In the wonder of my being.

Grip Golf

Arching through the air
Soaring balls open
The compressed wings
Of trapped minds.
They take flight
Over velvet greens
Releasing golfers
From built-up stress.
Inside in the clubhouse
Big egos surface
And tie strings
Around open wings,
Losing the freedom
Of outside wonder.

Stolen Birthright

They lived on the same hill,
But she never allowed her children
Access to their father's people.
Reared beneath her extended wing
They never savoured the paternal roots
Of a stifled parent.
With deprived vision
Will they never sense
Their lost inheritance?
Or in later years will they miss
The richness of double rooting?
Will they wonder why
They fly on one wing?

Release

Old resentments
A bag of bitterness
Inside the mind
Filtering hearing
Clouding vision
Holding prisoners
In the past.

Forgiveness
Oils hinges,
Softens
Rusted locks,
Opens doors
Of freedom
To walk
Into a new dawn.

Paradigm

Winds of life
Blow fragments of turmoil
Through cobwebs of fragility.
Some blow through
But others entangle
Delicate shreds,
Become immersed.
Perceptive changes.

Stolen Time

Winds calm;
Waves no longer
Crash on rocks.
Silent time
Going down
To rest in
The deep well
Of inner being.

Possession

Her insatiable need
Sucked out his soul.
She moved in
And looked out
In triumph
At herself.

Performing Monkey

Said stupid things,
Did stupid things,
But that was not me.
It was the other
Who takes over
When I get lost.

Let Me Out!

Stood around
In a sea of red wine,
And whirling words
Failed to mask
Bored minds.
Eyes sought
Over shoulders
Faces as valuable
As their TV
And news profile.

Needs

Give me space
To roll out my mind
So that I can open
Locked corners
Where lost thoughts
Are hidden.
I need time
In a quiet place
To walk around
The outer edges
Of my being,
To pick up
Fragmented pieces,
To put myself
Back together again.

Not Again!

There is always something wrong with you.
Your days an ongoing emergency.
You wallow in the drama of life,
Lurching from crisis to crisis.
You never find the quiet times
And all your performances
Demand a captive audience.

But we are growing weary
And are no longer impressed
With your theatrics.

Monsters

They slide into our home
Out through the TV screen.
They sit in the midst of us,
And we become of no consequence
To ourselves.

Return to Innishannon

When I am drained within
And the light
Which leads me on
Is quenched,
I come to this place
To be healed:
Its twin spires
Reach out to me
In a warm embrace
And I know
That I have come back
To my own place.
I have lived my life
Far from here
But I have taken
This little place
In the walled garden
Of my heart
To rekindle my tranquillity.
And when my life spring
Begins to fade
I make a pilgrimage
Back to my own place.

Roots

I have grown here
For many years,
Warm and safe
In my own place.
A lifetime of being here
Makes me feel secure;
My roots grow deep
Into the warm earth.
Now I am old,
My branches are tattered,
But still I would stay here
Because this is where I belong.
Do not dig me up:
The damage to my branches
Will ease me slowly from this place,
But pull up my roots
And my whole being will break.

Past

Turmoils of the past
Erupted
Blowing missiles
Into the peace
Of their lives.
Can they withstand
The assault,
Or will the past
Destroy the future?

All Wet Days

All her days were wet ones
And all her thoughts were sad;
Any time you met her
You would regret you had.
She'd depress you drip by drip
And leave you feeling low:
She is a wet-day woman
And will be always so.

The O'Connor Twins

We watch
Spellbound,
As they perform
Feats of skill
Beyond our suppressed
Expectations.
They reach, catch,
And shoot.
Then outrun the sliotar,
Arching into the air,
Swallows in upward curve.
Accurate and deadly
As swooping hawks
In full flight,
They grasp their prey
And jet it home
Between the posts.
The old man said,
"A safe pair of hands
Those twin lads have."
Birthed together and
Still bound by
Invisible strings,

They now play silent
Sliabh Luacra music
Across the turf
Of Croke Park.

Cork Hurlers

Across our GAA parks
We have watched
These fleeting deer
Play out battles
Of ferocious combat
In balletic swoops,
As warriors of old
Blending together
The art of aerial flight
And ground warfare,
They've plied skills
Of gladiatorial precision.

On their hurleys
They have borne on high
Minds of earthy souls,
Bearing them up into
Realms of unexplored delight.
Why do we feel the need
To now bring down these
Noble stags?

The Mysteries of the Rosary

She hung a rosary of troubles
Around my neck,
Dragged my mind into
The agony in the garden.
Around my gut
The scourging at the pillar.
With the crowning of thorns,
I fled her desolation.
Came into a sunlit garden
Where a man placed
Twelve eggs under a goose
In anticipation of golden goslings.
I celebrated his joy
Of the resurrection.

Get Up!

Dawn with a grey cowl
Around her head
Slashes greeting rain
Against my window,
Creating gloomy shadows
Around my bedroom.
I will have to dig deep
Inside my soul
For a good reason
To get out of bed.

Morning Shadows

My home in the morning
Is fusing with light,
The shadows are wearing
The coat-tails of night.
The softness of dawn
Is wrapping us round,
Softly eroding
Skulking night hound.

Morning Window

Clouds of lace
Trail across
The morning sky.
Billowing sheets
Of trailing elegance
Swirl white ballerinas
Across a blue stage.
No conductor in sight
Yet the performance
Flows as effortlessly
As the entry
Of the new day.

Morning Cobwebs

Early morning
Pools of silver,
Each tree a halo
Of webbed stars
Holding hands
Of shimmering chains
Shrouded in veils
Of silver mist
Reflecting the nature
Of the night.

Unwinding

Through a morning window,
Patch of blue in a grey sky.
Then the blue spreads and calms
The scudding grey clouds.
That patch of blue:
My soul
Needing time
To extend into my being.

Crash Me Not into a New Day

Let me unfold gently
Into the new day
As the sun calmly
Edging above the horizon
Before blazing into a dazzling dawn;
As the birds softly
Welcome the light
Before bursting into
The full dawn chorus;
As the cow rising
And stretching into
Her own body
Before bellowing
To her companions.

May I, too, slowly absorb,
Be calmed and centred
By the unfolding depths
Of this new day,
So that my inner being
Will dance in harmony
With whatever
It may bring.

Old Jugs

My room is full of old jugs—
Rose patterned, stone and lustre—
And in them are folded letters,
A soft baby shoe,
Key of a house where once I lived.
They are the urns of my life,
And I will go to sleep
Here in my attic room
Surrounded by my old jugs.

Cobweb of Old Age

Dear gentle soul,
Do not think
You are a burden.
In your love
You conceived them
And wove them
Into the fabric
Of your life,
Giving to them
All your strength.
The tide has turned,
They are the strong,
And you have your
Delicate threads
Caught in the cobweb
That is old age.
They would wrap
You in their strength,
Let them now
Because you can
Give them much
Of gentleness
And the wisdom
Of your time.

Please Cry

Don't stand dry-eyed
Around my grave:
Bathe me
In the love I gave.
Pour your tears
On the earth below
To soften the thud
As down I go.
The only funeral
I would fear:
Where ne'er a one
Would shed a tear.

The Scaffolding

When I am gone
And you who
Go through my things
Are left to sort,
Look kindly on
What I leave behind:
Jugs, pictures, books
And my beloved garden.
Maybe nothing valuable
In worldly eyes
But these are
Remnants of a life
That was filled
With beautiful moments,
And these things
Were the scaffolding.
Take them gently now
And lay them
Where they will
Be best loved.

Buried Free

When I die
Don't bury me
In a military style
Well-kept cemetery
Where everyone
Lies in rows
Of well organised
Parallel toes.
I'd rather be
On hilly ground
Where Mother Nature's
Abundance flowers;
Beneath a mark
Of natural stone
As bleached and grey
As will be my bones.
I could lie
Beneath a tree,
Whose whispering hair
Would shelter me.
Maybe long grass
And weeds would grow,
Better this
Than a disciplined row.

THE BOOKS OF ALICE TAYLOR

To School Through the Fields

"A very special book by a very special author . . . Read between the anecdotes and you discover a complete philosophy for our time, with invaluable lessons on everything from childcare and parenthood to the importance of the natural environment and the infinite variety of human nature." *Writer's Monthly*
ISBN 9780863220999

Quench the Lamp

"Infused with wit and lyricism, the story centers on the 1950s when the author and her friends were budding teenagers. Taylor describes the past vividly and without complaint as years of hard labor for herself, parents and siblings, making clear that the days also were full of fun shared with neighbors in the close-knit community." *Publishers Weekly*
ISBN 9780863221125

The Village

"What makes the story unique is Taylor's disarming style; she writes as though she were sitting next to you, at dusk, recounting the events of her week . . . Taylor has a knack for finding the universal truth in daily details." *Los Angeles Times*
ISBN 9780863221422

Country Days

"A rich patchwork of tales and reminiscences by the bestselling village postmistress from Co. Cork. Alice Taylor is a natural writer." *Daily Telegraph*
ISBN 9780863221682

The Night Before Christmas

"A nostalgic and loving look back to a family firmly rooted in tradition and humour. Whether the reader is in the teens or is a senior citizen, this book will charm and captivate." *Irish Independent*
ISBN 9780863221903

The Parish

"A pleasure to read; the author's amusing conversational style makes you feel that she is beside you telling the stories of her parish." *Irish Catholic*
ISBN 9780863223976

The Woman of the House

"An entrancing story written with much sensitivity and great depth of feeling, this is a delightful read." *Booklist*
ISBN 9780863222498

Across the River

"A story of land, conflict and family traditions . . . capturing the pulse and sinews of Irish rural life as no other author has done." *Clare Champion*
ISBN 9780863222856

House of Memories

"*House of Memories* shows her in her prime as a novelist." *Irish Independent*
ISBN 9780863223525